P9-CKX-596

Published by Creative Education
P.O. Box 227, Mankato, Minnesota 56002
Creative Education is an imprint of
The Creative Company
www.thecreativecompany.us

Design and production by The Design Lab
Art direction by Rita Marshall
Printed by Corporate Graphics
in the United States of America

Photographs by Corbis (Brandon D. Cole,
Michael & Patricia Fogden), Dreamstime (Hotduckz),
Getty Images (Tom Bean, DEA PICTURE LIBRARY,
George Grall, Thad Samuels Abell Ii, Roy Toft),
iStockphoto (Eric Isselée, Mark Kostich,
Ian McDonnell), Minden Pictures (Pete Oxford)

Library of Congress Cataloging-in-Publication Data
Bodden, Valerie.
Snakes / by Valerie Bodden.
p. cm. — (Amazing animals)
Includes bibliographical references and index.
Summary: A basic exploration of the appearance,
behavior, and habitat of snakes, a family of scaly
reptiles. Also included is a story from folklore
explaining why snakes do not have legs.
ISBN 978-1-58341-813-0
1. Snakes—Juvenile literature. I. Title. II. Series.
QL666.O6B685 2010
597.96—dc22   2009002717

CPSIA: 042412 PO1568

9 8 7

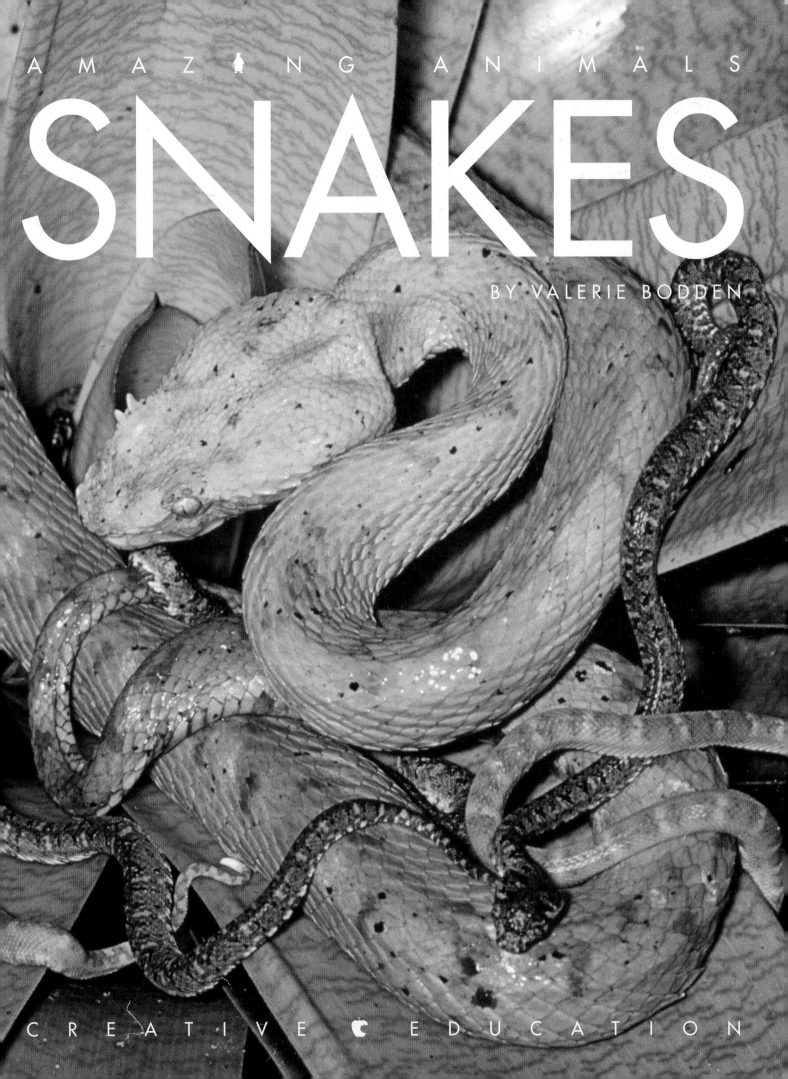

AMAZING ANIMALS
SNAKES

BY VALERIE BODDEN

CREATIVE EDUCATION

All snakes bend and twist their bodies to move

Snakes are long, thin **reptiles**. They do not have any legs. There are about 2,700 kinds of snakes in the world.

reptiles animals that have scales and a body that is always as warm or as cold as the air around it

A snake uses its tongue like other animals use noses

Snakes are covered with scales. The scales help protect the snakes. Snakes' scales come in lots of colors. Some are green or brown. Others are red or black. Snakes have a **forked** tongue. They use their tongue to pick up smells from the air.

forked split into two or more parts

Some snakes are tiny. They can be smaller than a worm. Other snakes are huge. They can be almost as long as a school bus! They can weigh much more than a grown-up man!

A snake called a boa is one of the biggest kinds

*Sea snakes live and swim
in the ocean like fish*

Snakes live all around the world. Some snakes live in the grass. Others live in forests. Some live in deserts. Some kinds of snakes even live in water.

deserts big, hot areas covered with sand

Snakes

Snakes eat many kinds of animals. Some snakes eat frogs or mice. Others eat birds. Some big snakes eat monkeys or deer. They swallow the animals in one gulp!

This snake is swallowing a big rat for dinner

Most snakes have about 3 to 16 babies at one time

Most mother snakes lay eggs. Baby snakes **hatch** out of the eggs. Other mother snakes give birth to live babies. Mother snakes do not take care of the baby snakes. As the baby snakes grow, they lose their old skin and grow new skin. Some snakes can live up to 40 years.

hatch   come out of an egg

Snakes spend much of the day lying around. If they are cold, they lie in the sun to warm up. If they get too hot, they crawl to a cooler place.

Snakes can hang in sunny tree branches to warm up

This snake wraps around
animals to kill them for food

Snakes spend some of their time looking for **prey**. When they find a prey animal, some snakes eat it alive. Other snakes kill their prey by squeezing it. Some snakes poison their prey when they bite it.

prey   animals that are eaten by other animals

Some people keep snakes as pets. Lots of people like to look at snakes in zoos. It is fun to watch these scaly animals bend and move!

Some small snakes that do not bite can be good pets

A Snake Story

Why don't snakes have legs? People on the **continent** of Africa used to tell a story about this. They said that some animals once had a farm. Someone stole the farm's food. The animals put tar on the ground to trap the thief. It was the snake! The animals pulled the snake out, but his legs stayed stuck in the tar. From then on, the snake had to crawl on his belly!

continent   one of Earth's seven big pieces of land

Read More

Macken, JoAnn Early. *Snakes*. Milwaukee: Weekly Reader Early Learning, 2002.

Stone, Lynn. *Wild World of Snakes*. Vero Beach, Fla.: Rourke, 2001.

Web Sites

Enchanted Learning: Snakes
http://www.enchantedlearning.com/painting/snakes.shtml
This site has lots of snake coloring pages.

Biology for Kids: Snakes
http://www.kidsbiology.com/animals-for-children.php?category=Snakes
This site has facts about many kinds of snakes.

Index